# Bottled Up Inside: African American Teens and Depression

(Revised Edition)

Rose Jackson-Beavers

and

Jermine D. Alberty

This book is a work of nonfiction. No names have been changed, no characters invented, no events fabricated. Although the case studies include incidents, characters, and dialogue that are products of the author's imagination and should not to be interpreted as real. Any resemblance to actual people, living or dead is entirely coincidental, except for those intended in the discussion. The information on depression is real.

This book is not intended as a substitute for the medical advice of physicians or mental health professionals. The reader should regularly consult a physician or mental health professional in matters relating to their health and particularly with respect to any symptoms that may require diagnosis or medical attention.

Prioritybooks Publications
P.O. Box 2535
Florissant, Mo 63033

Cover Designed by Chris House of InkosiDesigns

Back Cover Designed by Majaluk

Manufactured in the United States of America

Edited by LaMia Ashley @ lethalredpen31@yahoo.com
           Shelia Bell @ sheliawritesbooks@yahoo.com

Library of Congress 2016957806

ISBN 978-0-9792823-1-7
0-9792823-1-4

For information regarding discounts for bulk purchases, please contact Prioritybooks Publications at 1-314-306-2972 or rosbeav03@yahoo.com.

# Bottled Up Inside: African American Teens and Depression

(Revised Edition)

Published by Prioritybooks Publications
Missouri

# Contents

# DEDICATION

To all people who are suffering from trauma, help is available.

# EDNA PATTERSON-PETTY, MFA, MA, ATR

So many times, young people are afraid of their feelings and choose not to speak up. They take what they consider to be the easy way out, which turns out not so easy in the end. Youth are not always taught to talk about their feelings. If they are not comfortable talking about their feelings or own them, how can they express to an adult, or maybe even their peers, how they are feeling? When you are not taught to deal with your feelings, how can you even know what they are? Parents need to begin discussing feelings and emotions early with their children, but many of them may not even know how to themselves.

A book such as "Bottled Up Inside: African American Teens and Depression," is a significant step in acknowledging the problem of depression, however, some education has to take place for them to pick up the book. How many teens know what depression is? Oftentimes, signs of depression for some people are crying, not eating, and being isolated. What about those individuals that are hiding behind a mask and smiling all the time, trying to please others, getting good grades, etc., but later go home and die by suicide?

Our youth need to know that there are many forms of depression. Schools should also have some responsibility to get the information to their students. Depression is a community affair. It should be discussed in church groups, art groups, playgroups, etc. Youth need to know the difference between normal and abnormal feelings.

They should be able to communicate - if they get angry all the time - what their triggers are, how to handle their anger, who they're mad at, and why.

I have found in some young adults that I have counseled that they have deep-rooted anger and don't know why. They have a very short fuse. Sometimes, by peeling back the layers, they discover they were either sexually abused, bullied, neglected, etc., and this translates into depression. That person never identified with having depression because to them, anger is not a part of it.

Education on the symptoms of depression is key to getting children to open up and release themselves from that bottled-up feeling. We have to make it comfortable for them to feel free enough to talk. We have to seek out the youths that never talk, or the ones that sit quietly in the back of the classroom, never interacting, as well as the child that is considered a bully. We all have to do our part in dealing with, and preventing, the epidemic of suicide.

**Foreword by**

# JOE YANCEY, MPPH
## EXECUTIVE DIRECTOR | PLACES FOR PEOPLE

For the past four years, I have assisted in facilitating a support group for family members who have lost a loved one to gun violence. Unfortunately, the majority of participants are African American and, more often than not, mothers, who have lost sons, though we also have other family members. One night, a sixteen-year-old brother whose cousin had been murdered shared the following statement with the group: "We can't be human." When I asked what he meant by that, he said, "We aren't able to show our emotions or feelings, because if we do, we are seen as weak and become a 'target'.

In their informative and must-read book, "Bottled Up Inside: African American Teens and Depression," Rose Jackson-Beavers and Rev. Jermine D. Alberty directly address the health-threatening issue of the stigma around the issues of mental health and emotional well-being that are so prevalent in the African-American community. What was profoundly evident to me in the statement that this young man shared is that this stigma is so pervasive among our young men, that succumbing to the emotions of sadness, grief or anxiety could literally threaten one's safety.

We are a strong and resilient people, having survived slavery, indentured servitude, Jim Crow, other legally-sanctioned injustices, and institutional and structural racism. However, we too often fail to recognize and address the threat that the constant, toxic stress, that is so much a part of these ongoing struggles, plays in the basic vulnerability of each of our families, our communities, and us over time. Trauma and toxic stress, particularly experienced by children and adolescents on a fairly constant basis, we now know from the multiple replications of the Adverse Childhood Experience (ACE) studies, too often lead to depression, anxiety, substance use, and a significant increase in vulnerability to chronic physical health conditions as that child grows up and moves into adulthood.

The fact of the matter is that our black children living, too often, in communities of concentrated poverty, are at immediate risk for developing depression, anxiety and other mental health disorders. Often, to feel better, they may begin self-medicating their symptoms with alcohol and drugs or engaging in other risky and dangerous behavior that threatens their overall health, well-being, and in some cases, life. This book is an important step in bringing this threat out of the shadows and into the sunlight.

The good news is that through this book, Ms. Jackson-Beavers and Rev. Alberty provide parents, other caretakers, and all involved in the lives of our children with very concrete and actionable steps we can take to protect and educate them as they go from childhood through the very challenging teen years. This book is not written from the perspective of an academic scholar or clinician, but rather a courageous gift from the authors gleaned through their own, personal lived experiences.

Jackson-Beavers and Alberty provide specific recommendations of things we, as parents and caretakers, must be aware of, in regards to the signs of depression, anxiety or other mental health disorders. They also provide us with specific actions we can take and resources that are available if we believe that a teenager needs help and support. I have been a mental health professional and administrator for almost 40 years, but was at a loss when I recognized that my son was dealing with depression as a teenager and my daughter was dealing with significant anxiety as a seven-year-old. Through those experiences, I have become aware of, and used many of the techniques and recommendations that this book suggests, and found them to be extremely helpful.

I highly recommend this book as required reading for any

adult who is involved in the life of African-American teenagers today. The sooner that the disorders focused on in this book are treated appropriately, the better the prognosis is for healing, as with any medical disorder, and result in an emotionally-healthy life. For the past four years, I have assisted in facilitating a support group for family members who have lost a loved one to gun violence. Unfortunately, the majority of participants are African American and, more often than not, mothers, who have lost sons, though we also have other family members. One night, a sixteen-year-old brother whose cousin had been murdered shared the following statement with the group: "We can't be human." When I asked what he meant by that, he said, "We aren't able to show our emotions or feelings, because if we do, we are seen as weak and become a 'target'.

In their informative and must-read book, "Bottled Up Inside: African American Teens and Depression," Rose Jackson-Beavers and Rev. Jermine D. Alberty directly address the health-threatening issue of the stigma around the issues of mental health and emotional well-being that are so prevalent in the African-American community. What was profoundly evident to me in the statement that this young man shared is that this stigma is so pervasive among our young men, that succumbing to the emotions of sadness, grief or anxiety could literally threaten one's safety.

We are a strong and resilient people, having survived slavery, indentured servitude, Jim Crow, other legally-sanctioned injustices, and institutional and structural racism. However, we too often fail to recognize and address the threat that the constant, toxic stress, that is so much a part of these ongoing struggles, plays in the basic vulnerability of each of our families, our communities, and us over time. Trauma and toxic stress, particularly experienced by children and adolescents on a fairly constant basis, we now know from the multiple replications of the Adverse Childhood Experience (ACE) studies, too often lead to depression, anxiety, substance use, and a significant increase in vulnerability to chronic physical health conditions as that child grows up and moves into adulthood.

The fact of the matter is that our black children living, too often, in communities of concentrated poverty, are at immediate risk for developing depression, anxiety and other mental health disorders. Often, to feel better, they may begin self-medicating their symptoms with alcohol and drugs or engaging in other risky and dangerous behavior that threatens their overall health, well-being, and in some cases, life. This book is an important step in bringing this threat out of the shadows and into the sunlight.

The good news is that through this book, Ms. Jackson-Beavers and Rev. Alberty provide parents, other caretakers, and all involved in the lives of our children with very concrete and actionable steps we can take to protect and educate them as they go from childhood through the very challenging teen years. This book is not written from the perspective of an academic scholar or clinician, but rather a courageous gift from the authors gleaned through their own, personal lived experiences.

Jackson-Beavers and Alberty provide specific recommendations of things we, as parents and caretakers, must be aware of, in regards to the signs of depression, anxiety or other mental health disorders. They also provide us with specific actions we can take and resources that are available if we believe that a teenager needs help and support. I have been a mental health professional and administrator for almost 40 years, but was at a loss when I recognized that my son was dealing with depression as a teenager and my daughter was dealing with significant anxiety as a seven-year-old. Through those experiences, I have become aware of, and used many of the techniques and recommendations that this book suggests, and found them to be extremely helpful.

I highly recommend this book as required reading for any adult who is involved in the life of African-American teenagers today. The sooner that the disorders focused on in this book are treated appropriately, the better the prognosis is for healing, as with any medical disorder, and result in an emotionally-healthy life.

# Introduction

The youth of today are faced with numerous obstacles. It's amazing how they can keep so much bottled up inside. The pressures of today can often be so troubling, that they are shaken to their very core, and may find themselves bursting from the seams from all the stuff they are keeping inside.

For many of these youth, if their struggles and challenges are not addressed, it could develop into mental illness. It is sobering to know that approximately 20% of adolescents have a diagnosable mental health disorder[1] . Between 25% and 33% forgo needed care, and many others lack access.

In these staggering numbers, African-American youth are represented who, due to stigma, may not receive a diagnosis or receive treatment for their mental illness.

When one takes into account the historical adversity, which includes slavery, sharecropping, and race-based exclusion from health, educational, social, and economic resources, it translates into socioeconomic disparities experienced by African Americans today. Socioeconomic status, in turn, is linked to mental health. People who are impoverished, homeless, incarcerated, or have substance abuse problems are at higher risk for poor mental health.

It is no coincidence that African Americans go undiagnosed with depression and many other mental health conditions. In this community, the stigma associated with depression keeps individual from seeking help. As African Americans, we all must understand that depression is real and that our children are not immune to being depressed. Depression is a health problem and not a personal weakness. We must help people to understand that just as the physical body can become sick, so

1 Kessler, R. C.; Berglund, P.; Demler, O.; Jin, R.; Walters, E. E. 2005. Life-time Prevalence and Age-of-onset Distribution of DSM-IV Disorders in the National Co-morbidity Survey Replication. Archives of General Psychiatry 62: 593-602

can the mind.

Helping teens means increasing their knowledge and awareness about mental health issues and the effects of these illnesses. If we are to help teenagers, we must understand the symptoms of depression and aid those teens who may be depressed in getting the medical attention they need.

Rose Jackson-Beavers is an advocate for teens and works in close collaboration with faith communities and other organizations to encourage and support young people to never give up. She has had encounters that could have changed her life forever. In this book, she will share her experiences and how caring adults in her life served as protective factors.

Rev. Jermine Alberty is a National trainer for Mental Health First Aid, pastor, and champion of mental health literacy. In November 2015, he received a message from his daughter that he hoped he would have never received - his son had attempted suicide and was taken to an inpatient unit for evaluation. In this book, he will share the journey of his son's road to recovery and an intervention strategy he developed to help him maintain his wellness.

We hope this book will serve as a guide to help curious adults learn more about mental illness; in particular, depression, and how to help the youth they encounter daily.

In this book, the reader will learn how to assist youth dealing with the turmoil of adolescence, gain an understanding of depression, identify potential risk factors and protective factors, and learn an intervention to help youth in non-crisis and crisis situations.

# Chapter 1

## MENTAL HEALTH CHALLENGE & MENTAL ILLNESS

Before we can address depression, we need to understand that youth experience challenges that often impact their mental well-being. So, what does a mental health challenge mean? It is a broader term to include both mental illnesses and clusters of symptoms that are not severe enough to meet the criteria of a mental illness/disorder.

Most people believe that mental disorders are rare and "happen to someone else," when, in fact, mental disorders are common and widespread. An estimated 54 million Americans suffer from some form of mental disorder in a given year.

Most families are not prepared to cope with learning their loved one has a mental illness. It can be physically and emotionally trying, and can make them feel vulnerable to the opinions and judgments of others.

If you think you or someone you know may have a mental or emotional challenge, it is important to remember there is hope and help.

### What is mental illness?

A mental illness is a condition that affects a person's thinking, feeling or mood. Such conditions may affect someone's ability to relate to others and function each day. Each person will have different experiences, even people with the same diagnosis.[2]

There are more than 200 classified forms of mental illness. Some of the more common disorders are: depression, bipolar disorder, dementia, schizophrenia, and anxiety disorders. Symptoms may include changes in mood, personality, personal

---

2  https://www.nami.org/Learn-More/Mental-Health-Conditions

3

habits, and/or social withdrawal.[3]

Mental health problems may be related to excessive stress, due to a particular situation or series of events. As with cancer, diabetes, and heart disease, mental illnesses are often physical as well as emotional and psychological. [4]

Mental illness may be caused by a reaction to environmental stresses, genetic factors, biochemical imbalances, or a combination of these. With proper care and treatment, many individuals learn to cope or recover from a mental illness or emotional disorder.

The best way to prevent mental health challenges from getting worse is to recognize symptoms early and seek professional help.

Many mental health challenges and disorders can be treated successfully. When the signs are recognized early, that person can get started on the path to a full recovery.[5]

When talking about signs and symptoms of mental illness, the question might be what should we look for. Before we can answer that question, let's first define what a sign/symptom is. A sign is what you might see in a person, while a symptom is what the person is experiencing. Remember, if you are not a mental health professional, it is not your job to diagnose the young person.

It is especially important to pay attention to sudden changes in thoughts and behaviors like the ones below:

- Confused thinking

- Prolonged depression (sadness or irritability)

- Feelings of extreme highs and lows

3  http://www.fultoncountyga.gov/bhdd-symptoms-a-warning-signs

4  http://www.mentalhealthamerica.net/recognizing-warning-signs

5  http://www.mentalhealthamerica.net/recognizing-warning-signs

- Excessive fears, worries, and anxieties

- Social withdrawal

- Dramatic changes in eating or sleeping habits

- Strong feelings of anger

- Strange thoughts (delusions)

- Seeing or hearing things that aren't there hallucinations)

- Growing inability to cope with daily problems and activities

- Suicidal thoughts

- Numerous, unexplained physical ailments

- Substance use [6]

If you are concerned about that young person, seek help for him or her. The earlier you intervene, the better outcome the youth will have in their recovery.

In the next chapter, you'll learn about a serious mental illness - depression. Did you know that among black youth about 7.9% meet the diagnosis for major depression?

---

6 http://www.mentalhealthamerica.net/recognizing-warning-signs

**Chapter 2**

# THE FACTS ABOUT DEPRESSION

The National Institute of Mental Health describes depression as more than the blues or the blahs.[7] Depression is a brain disorder that affects the way a person thinks, feels, or acts. It is more than having a bad moment or a bad day. It is more than dealing with the loss of a family member, friend, or pet.

Depression is more than the average fluctuation of feelings. There are many times in our lives when we feel sad or discouraged about problems that may trouble or sadden us. Depression is not a weakness or a character flaw.

When these feelings last for more than two weeks and occur along with other symptoms, the person may be suffering from clinical depression which we discuss later in this chapter. It is important to note that teens suffering from clinical depression cannot just snap out of feeling sad. Did you know that:

- One in every 33 children may have depression.[8]

- Up to 2.5% of children and up to 8.3% of adolescents in the U.S. suffer from depression.[9]

- Children under stress, who experience loss, or who have attention, learning, or conduct disorders are at a higher risk for depression.[10]

There is no single cause of depression and it often involves many factors. Those factors could include the following:

- Family history

---

7   National Institute of Mental Health

8   Center for Mental Health Services, U.S. Department of Health and Human Services. (1996)

9   National Institute of Mental Health, "Depression research at the National Institute of Mental Health," updated April 13, 1999.

10   American Academy of Child and Adolescent Psychiatry: "The Depressed Child." Facts for Families Fact Sheet Series, Accessed Sept. 1999.

- Major life changes

- Major illness such as: heart attacks, cancer or stroke

- Use of alcohol or other drugs can lead to or worsen depression

- Certain medications, when used alone or in combination, can cause side effects like the symptoms of depression

Depression is also believed to be caused by changes in the brain's chemistry. The chemicals in the brain are referred to as neurotransmitters, which assist in transmitting messages between nerve cells in the brain. It is said that there is an imbalance or a deficient level of neurotransmitters (the brain's chemical substances) such as serotonin and norepinephrine that could cause a person to become depressed.

**What are some other reasons teens might become depressed?**

- Peer pressure - feeling like they don't belong

- Bullying – being repeatedly picked on

- Poor relationships – always fighting with siblings and friends

- Dealing with grief - losing a loved one

- Stress - dealing with the ups and downs of daily life

- Dealing with divorce - believing they had something to do with their parents splitting up

- Substance abuse - Addiction can affect all members of a family.

**Who is affected by depression?**

- Middle age people

- Older people

- Young adults

- Adolescents

- Children

Women are more likely to be diagnosed with depression than men. This may be the result of biological differences. It could also be influenced by the fact that women are more likely to seek help for depression, making it easier to document this information.

Depression can be a big problem for teens. Research shows about seven percent are affected by the disease, which can persist into adulthood. It is important to identify depression early in youth because untreated depression could increase the risk for suicide. In the African-American community, the topic of depression is being discussed more. This may be due to the increase of suicides among African-American teens.

One study found that among Black youth 3.2% reported some suicidal thoughts in the past year; and 1.4% reported attempting suicide (Joe et al., 2009).[11]

This may seem like a small number. However, suicide is the third leading cause of death among Black youth (Lincoln et al., 2012).[12]

Many African-American teens are reluctant to seek help because they do not want to be labeled as *crazy*. However, if we

---

11 Joe, S., Baser, R. S., Neighbors, H. W., Caldwell, C. H., & Jackson, J. S. (2009). 12-month and lifetime prevalence of suicide attempts among black adolescents in the National Survey of American Life. Journal of the American Academy of Child & Adolescent Psychiatry, 48(3), 271-282.

12 Lincoln, K. D., Taylor, R. J., Chatters, L. M., & Joe, S. (2012). Suicide, negative interaction and emotional support among black Americans. Social psychiatry and psychiatric epidemiology, 47(12), 1947-1958.

discuss depression more openly, the negative connotations associated with getting help can be changed. This begins with education and gaining an understanding of the different types of mood disorders in which depression occurs.

What are the types of depression?

*Mental illnesses are defined by the Diagnostic and Statistical Manual of Mental Disorders (DSM). This publication describes the standard criteria for different types of psychiatric disorders.*

*A common rule is that a person's symptoms either cause 1) significant distress, or 2) impair one's functioning (e.g. work, school, relationships). Also, these depressive symptoms are not caused by a medical condition or substance (e.g. medication, drug).* [13]

*Three mood disorders that include depression is Clinical depression also known as major depression (MD) or major depressive disorder (MDO), Persistent Depressive Disorder and bipolar disorder which includes depression and mania.* [14]

Clinical depression is a serious health problem. It affects more than feelings. It changes physical health, appearance, behavior, academic performance, and social behavior. It also has an impact on a person's ability to handle everyday pressures, decisions, and outlooks on life. [15]

## What are the basic facts about clinical depression?

Clinical depression affects more than 19 million people per year. It is reported that one-fourth of all women and one-eighth of all men will suffer at least one episode or occurrence of depression in their lifetime. Depression can affect people of all ages but is less common in teens than adults. Every year, three to five percent of teenagers experience clinical depression.[16]

13  http://www.depression-help-resource.com/types-of-depression.htm

14  http://www.depression-help-resource.com/types-of-depression.htm

15  http://www.depression-help-resource.com/types-of-depression.htm

16  http://www.depression-help-resource.com/types-of-depression.htm

An example of this statistic could look like this: If you were with four friends, at least one of them could be suffering from clinical depression.

*Clinical Depression is more common than people think. Based on an article written by Erlanger A. Turner Ph.D., who states that:*

- *Major depression occurs in about 9% of teens ages 12 to 17.*

- *Depression is more common in girls (13.7%) than boys (4.7%).*

- *Among Black youth about 7.9% meet diagnosis for major depression.*

There are symptoms that occur with major depression that lasts for most of the day, nearly every day for at least two weeks. A symptom must either be 1) depressed mood, or 2) a noticeable decrease in interest or pleasure in all or most activities. There are additional symptoms that may be present.[17]

Such as:

- Always moving or slowing down associated with mental tension

- Tired or loss of energy

- A feeling of worthless or guilt

- Problems sleeping or too much sleeping

- Thoughts about death or suicide, trying to attempt suicide or having a specific plan to die by suicide

---

17  http://www.depression-help-resource.com/types-of-depression.htm

- Unable to think or concentrate

- Weight gain/weight loss/increase in appetite

It is important that the reader understands that these symptoms could be typical adolescent behavior. The teens I talked to exhibited many of these symptoms. They suffered from the desire to do nothing and spent many hours sleeping. There were times they would sit in the dark and keep the shades drawn. They didn't want any sunlight to come through the windows. Often, they didn't eat because they lacked an appetite. They were tired, or when trying to complete a task, lacked focus, became tired easily and some eventually gave up.

This doesn't mean that they have a disorder it is when the symptoms begin to impair the teens ability to function that you should seek help for them.

Another disorder that includes depression is Persistent Depressive Disorder is also referred to as dysthymia. This is when a person is constantly in a depressed mood. This mood can last up to two years and has at least two or more symptoms. They are:

- Problems sleeping or increase in sleeping

- Suffers from low self-esteem

- Decrease or increase in eating

- Unable to make decisions, difficulty concentrating

- Lack of energy, tiredness or fatigue

- Feeling hopeless

Symptoms do not occur for more than two months at a time. This type of depression is described as having persistent but less severe depressive symptoms than Major Depression.[18]

18  http://www.depression-help-resource.com/types-of-depression.htm

The last mood disorder we will discuss is Manic depression also known as bipolar disorder. This type of depression includes periods of mania and depression. The person can go between these two states. It can be rapid or only mania, which can be present without any depressive episodes. A manic episode consists of a persistent, elevated, or irritable mood that is extreme, which lasts for at least one week.

At least three (four if only irritable mood) other features are also present:

- Inflated self-esteem or self-importance

- Decreased need for sleep

- More talkative than usual or compelled to keep talking

- Racing thoughts or ideas

- Easily distracted

- Increase in goal-oriented activity (social, work, school, sexual) or excessive movement

- Excessive involvement in potentially risky, pleasurable behavior (e.g. over spending, careless, sexual activity.) Symptoms can be severe enough to warrant hospitalization to prevent harm to self or others or include psychotic features (e.g. hallucinations, delusions).[19]

A teen I encountered during my days as a facilitator in a social service organization exhibited manic depression symptoms in my presence. I had scheduled a meeting to discuss setting goals with this young woman, and before I knew what was happening, she started mimicking my behavior. Whatever I did, from crossing my legs to writing on a pad, she did the same. When she began repeating my exact words, I knew I was dealing with

---

19  http://www.depression-help-resource.com/types-of-depression.htm

13

someone with a mental illness. I guided her through a process, without being able to correctly identify what was happening. When a senior manager passed my door, I invited him in. He figured out quickly what was happening and contacted mental health services, and an ambulance was called. The reason we had to get help is because her behavior changed quickly, and her actions became extremely delusional. She believed she was me.

Although I was unable to obtain more detailed information due to confidentiality issues, I did learn from the teen that she was diagnosed with manic depression and bipolar disorder. She further stated she had stopped taking her medication because she was not crazy.

This is another reason I feel teenagers need to understand that there is nothing wrong with getting help when they have issues or become ill, or need to take medications or receive counseling to address a mental health issue. Neglecting to seek help can put the depressed person, their family members, friends, or others in jeopardy because of the depressed person's mental state.

Mental health is not an illness but specific mental health issues are. Like any other disease, mental health issues require a professional who specializes in the area to help. There is absolutely nothing wrong with obtaining help. No one should be ashamed of being sick. Like cancer, diabetes, and other illnesses, there is help for individuals who are diagnosed with mental health issues. We pray for and encourage people who are ill to get better. We must do the same with our young people, as well as anyone who is suffering from mental health issues.

Teenagers are extremely vulnerable, because of the many social ills they face. Many children and young people are bullied, put down for being different, suffering from family issues, suffering from trauma, and cannot handle much more stress in their lives.

As adults, we must provide resources and encouragement to let our young people know that recovery is possible. Recovery begins with reducing the stigma about mental illness, as it is essential. As caring adults, we can make a difference and be a protective factor.

## Chapter 3

# TRAUMA, A POWERFUL RISK FACTOR DEALING WITH THE TURMOIL OF ADOLESCENCE

According to youth.gov, a risk factor can be defined as "a characteristic at the biological, psychological, family, community, or cultural level that precedes and is associated with a higher likelihood of problem outcomes."[20]

Trauma is one of the most powerful risk factors that increases the risk of developing a mental illness. One thing that seems to be constant when we look at why many African-American teens are suffering in several areas of their lives, is a risk factor known as trauma.

What is trauma? *"Trauma is an emotional response to a terrible event like an accident, rape, or natural disaster. Immediately after the event, shock and denial are typical. Long-term reactions include: unpredictable emotions, flashbacks, strained relationships, and even physical symptoms like headaches or nausea. While these feelings are normal, some people have difficulty moving on with their lives. (http://www.apa.org/topics/trauma/)* [21]

Exposure to traumatic experiences is one of the reasons many African-American teens experience depression. It is a fact that African-American teens are dealing with many challenges. These challenges include: broken homes, absent fathers, unemployment, being undereducated, hopelessness, being bullied, and living fearfully in their own neighborhoods. It is hard not to feel sad when your world seems to be falling apart around you.

Facing such challenges, one could see how a youth might experience symptoms of depression; yet, many teens may never

---

20  O'Connell, M. E., Boat, T., & Warner, K. E.. (2009). Preventing mental, emotional, and behavioral disorders among young people: Progress and possibilities.

21  http://www.apa.org/topics/trauma/

receive a diagnosis or treatment. When youth go untreated for depression, many teenagers spiral out of control. Not understanding they could be suffering from a behavioral health issue... Not understanding that what they are experiencing could be an illness, some might mistake their behavior as simply being deviant. Some youth may mask their problems by consuming drugs and/or alcohol, while continuing to spiral out of control. If their negative behavior is not checked, they could get in trouble and become lost in the judicial system. The question we must ask ourselves is: how do we help young people who may discover they are suffering from behavioral problems?

First, we need to understand the risk factors that put them at risk. Our children have experienced trauma in many forms. One, in particular, is abuse. It can be emotional, physical, or mental abuse.

Trauma is something that has been experienced by young people in many ways. When a child experiences trauma in their young life, and it is not addressed through counseling or discussion, feelings of inadequacy can linger into adulthood. It is so important to get help for anyone who has suffered any form of trauma.

One of many effects of trauma is grief. Grief that is not processed can lead to depression, and anxiety. It can also lead to self-medication by using alcohol or other drugs.

In the upcoming chapters, we will define grief, and explain the development of grief and how to process it.

## Chapter 4

# WHAT IS GRIEF AND HOW DO PEOPLE GRIEVE?

Merriam-Webster's dictionary describes grief as a deep sadness caused by death, or trouble or annoyance. When someone you love dies, the pain can become unbearable. Imagine if you are a young person and you lose your mother, father, or a sibling. Many of our children are experiencing this kind of traumatic grief in their lives.

In some African-American communities, people we know and love die daily as a result of high crime. From one day to the next, you're not sure if your loved one will survive this current epidemic.

As an adult, how would you feel if you lost your spouse or child? How would you feel if you walked out into your neighborhood and had to dodge bullets and people who may do you harm to you for simply being in the wrong place at the wrong time? That is what is happening in many African-American communities. Young people are dying fast, and there seems to be no stopping or slowing it down. Crime is at an all-time high, and it takes nothing to see a dead body lying out in the street.

After experiencing such pain, experts expect that the person would become traumatized. In many homes, some have seen so much death, yet they don't pay attention to how it affects them or their family members. For communities that experience daily deaths, break-ins, robberies, rapes, and day-after-day pain, this may manifest itself in that person's heart and head.

They may not be able to sleep at night. They may want to sleep during the day. They want the house darkened. They refuse to see loved ones and friends. They stop doing the things they once loved. They cry about anything, or they lose their appetite.

Grief affects each of us differently. Over time, if the person affected does not take care of himself, grief will take over his or her life. This is why it is important to help the person who is grieving.

If a kid is killed and he was your child's friend or playmate, you should demand counseling from the school they attend. The same goes for a person suffering from a family loss. Get the person help. There are many free services available to do so. Whatever you do, do not allow the person to grieve indefinitely. They must talk about their pain, and some may have to take medication. The thing is they must get help.

Don't take for granted that someone experiencing grief will eventually get over it; especially, if the death of people you know continues to happen regularly. For instance, in some African-American communities, there are many teenagers and young adults being gunned down. Almost daily, you hear the story of another person losing their life Most people think because this happens so often, people can easily get over it, when the truth is that you never get over death.

Think about this—if death keeps happening in your neighborhood, at what point do you get a chance to stop grieving? Sometimes people may think you have become immune to death and the pain is so normal that you can function. However, the truth is traumatic experiences have a way of hanging on. It's like the root of a tree. If you don't deal with the problem, it becomes entangled, and the roots spread all over. That's how trauma is for people. If it is not dealt with, the problem festers and grows, gaining more negative energy, unless it is addressed through counseling or talking.

Parents should allow their children to grieve but also get the help they need to deal with this issue. If your child is experiencing sadness and cannot seem to move forward, seek help immediately.

People grieve in many different ways. Some people may start off feeling very little emotion, but as time moves on, they become extremely emotional. Other times, they may start off sad, filled with emotions, and as time moves on, they seem to get better.

A good way to tell what is happening to a person after a loss is to have them talk about the death that occurred. Another way is to encourage the person to document their feelings in a journal.

- These are some common ways people grieve:

- They cannot believe the person is dead

- Afraid another love one will die

- They become angry at the person, or at God

- Cannot stop thinking about the death

- Cannot do much of anything, lacks energy and desire

- Feelings of sadness all the time

- Cries all the time

- Wants to die to be with the person

- They avoid places or things the person who died attended or spent time around while they were alive.

**Chapter 5**

# HOW DOES GRIEF PLAY A PART IN DEPRESSION?

Grief plays a significant role in depression in many children and young people who may have lost a loved one. Think about this. If an adult loses a spouse or a child, the pain is unbearable. Sometimes, we lose ourselves emotionally because we are so sad. Our hearts hurt from such a loss, and we feel as if we cannot go on.

For a child, or young teen, that pain may be too awful to deal with, and they may fall deep into depression. Many children and youth do not understand the signs or symptoms of depression, so they suffer. Too many people keep the pain inside because they may believe that others do not care or understand, therefore, they end up grieving alone.

To help someone who is grieving, encourage them to talk about their loss. If they will not talk to you, they have to talk to someone else.

There are five stages of grieving. Learn what they are and determine if your loved one is going through any of the stages. The stages are:

- Denial

- Anger

- Bargaining

- Depression

- Acceptance

In the first stage - *denial*, people tend to believe that the death is not true, that it did not happen. The want to believe the person did not die. They cannot accept the loss. They think, or say, "That's not true," or "I don't believe you."

Second stage - *anger*, the person that is grieving becomes angry that the person went away. "How dare they die and leave me?" they may ask.

Third stage - *bargaining*, the grieving person bargains with God or anyone to bring the person back. They would trade places, if only their loved one could come back. They would quickly take their place."

Fourth stage - *depression*, the grieving person is sad all the time. I have watched some young people refuse to associate with others, stay in the house, and keep the curtains closed. They are too sad to function normally.

Fifth stage - *acceptance*. The grieving person has accepted the loss and begins to move forward to other things.

It's important to understand that not everyone will go through each of these stages. Some people will skip one or two, while others may experience each stage in no certain order.

Remember: Grieving is different for each person. It may last a week, a month, or longer, depending on the person. Paying attention to the grieving person and asking questions is key, in order to know what you should do to help the person.

If you believe someone is depressed, talk to them. Ask them how they are feeling and be honest and let them know what you are thinking. People need honesty to handle their situation. If they feel you are not compassionate, they will not listen to you. To get people the help they need, be open and show concern. Let them know that they are going to be okay and can live a normal life, which may include having to take prescribed medication.

If at all possible, do not allow the person to suffer and under no circumstances should you push them down deeper because of your own beliefs and disbeliefs.

# Chapter 6
## WHAT SHOULD A PERSON DO WHO IS GRIEVING?

You may want to know what a person should do who is grieving. A good idea is for the person to join a grief support group.

It's hard to talk to others when you are grieving. It may be difficult to share your true feelings when you are grieving. When I lost my oldest brother to cancer, the pain was immense. He was diagnosed in April 1995 with throat cancer, and by the end of July, he was gone. Although I spent as much time with him as I could, his death devastated me. It was sudden and unexpected, when it happened. I found myself not wanting to talk to people about it. When I discussed his death, it made the pain too fresh. Discussing it made me emotional and all I could do was cry. However, I could listen to others share their memories of him.

As a result of my personal experiences, I learned the significance of support groups. With support groups, you can listen without judgment. You hear others; and, somehow, knowing that others are healing helps you feel that maybe down the line, you will get better, too. Being with people living your experience is healing. You believe they understand your pain. You're hoping that you too will heal. Although it seems you never will, being around others with shared experiences helps.

You can find support groups in your area by contacting various agencies, churches, hospitals, or funeral homes. Visit your national mental health literacy and advocacy organizations like the National Alliance for Mental Illness site, www.nami.org , Mental Health America http://www.mentalhealthamerica.net/ and look for local group in your community.

Another suggestion for grieving is to *seek counseling* through a therapist or experienced grief counselors. They can help you overcome obstacles and be the listening ear you need during your time of grief. These trained individuals can help you or the grieving person wade through your emotions.

- Talk to family and friends

This is the time to be honest about your feelings. You're hurting, and it's understandable. People who love you want to help but they don't know how. Tell them what you need. Be open and allow them to help you. They love you, and you love your friends and family, so allow them to be the shoulder you need to release your pain.

- Lean on your faith

When people are grieving, it's easy to feel like your faith or a higher being has failed you. When you feel this way, seek guidance from your faith or spiritual leader and seek support from your faith or spiritual community.

Whatever approach one takes to manage grief, finding support is essential.

# Chapter 7

# CARING ADULTS: POWERFUL PROTECTIVE FACTORS

Oftentimes, when a teen goes through a traumatic experience of grief, and it is not addressed, or the people who are supposed to protect the teen, accuse them, and treat the kid indifferent, this could lead to a serious problem. If a child comes to you for help, and they walk away feeling as if they did something wrong, that kind of negative experience will linger in the child's psyche long after the incident has occurred. That denial leaves the victim feeling alone, lost and not important enough for someone to protect them.

In order to help our youth, we must ensure that they are protected. This protection can happen in the form of protective factors.

According to youth.gov, *a protective factor can be defined as "a characteristic at the biological, psychological, family, or community (including peers and culture) level that is associated with a lower likelihood of problem outcomes or that reduces the negative impact of a risk factor on problem outcomes."*[22]

One of the most significant protective factors that a youth can have is feeling close to at least one adult.

This was a key factor that helped the author, Rose Jackson-Beavers, as a youth growing up. She had engaged parents in her home that recognized when she needed help. It made it easier for her to deal with several, traumatic experiences she encountered as a pre-teen.

When a loved one decided to touch her inappropriately, she

---

22  O'Connell, M. E., Boat, T., & Warner, K. E.. (2009). Preventing mental, emotional, and behavioral disorders among young people: Progress and possibilities.

was able to go to her mother and talk to her about what happened. Her mother went to the perpetrator and discussed the issue with him. Although he denied it, his family believed he touched her and they dealt with him accordingly.

What she received from that experience was a form of talk therapy and the belief that she was okay and that her parents believed and supported her. What that did for her was remove the guilt and shame. She understood that she was not the problem. As a result, she was able to deal with the traumatic event and receive help and support. Our teens need this same support, when they experience traumatic experiences. They need a caring adult that will hear them out and support them and get them the help they need.

Another negative experience that caused trauma in her life, which could have proved to harm her in the future had it not it been handled immediately, involved an act of molestation at a swimming pool at the age of 11 years old. Rose loved to go swimming every day in the summer. She loved the water and looked forward to spending time with her friends.

One day, an older guy that she hadn't seen before was in the water. As she swam out to the deeper end, he began to grope her and tried to pull her swimming bottoms off. As she fought him, she went under the water. She was screaming and this frightened him. He swam off and left the pool. The lifeguard came to check on her and she told him what happened but the guy had left. She told her brothers and described him. Her brothers looked for the guy but didn't find him. They stayed with her and encouraged her to continue to swim. They helped her understand that it was not her issue but the act of a boy heading for trouble.

They protected her the entire summer. She felt secure and safe. This protection that she felt is one that we need to offer to all of our youth.

For Rose, her faith in God at a young age was quintessential to her maintaining wellness. Research shows that spirituality can be an important protective factor for youth.

# Chapter 8

# SPIRITUALITY: AN IMPORTANT PROTECTIVE FACTOR

Spirituality can be a potential protective factor for children and adolescents exposed to stressful life events.

Before some African Americans will seek outside help to address their issues of sadness or loneliness, or even to address potential mental illness, **they will seek help from God and the church**. That's great! In order for the church or the pastors to help them, they must be informed about mental health, where the resources are, and how to access the resources so they can provide the support needed for that person.

Too often, people in the church believe that God is the only answer. Just pray is what you may hear. In all honesty, that is not a bad idea. Many of our youth are spiritual, believe in a higher power, and lean on God and prayer.

There is nothing wrong with prayer. God does answer prayers, but we should also encourage our young people to seek professional help. However, that encouragement is often met with cynicism. If you ask some people in the African-American community what they think about counseling, you may hear, "People who need counseling are crazy." It is important that we equip faith communities to recognize this stigma that often leads to discrimination. This equipping must begin with our faith leaders.

In the African American community, faith leaders are often our greatest help in times of need. Hurt people often tend to keep their pain on the inside, believing they will get better. If they talk to anyone, it might be their pastors.

Faith leaders have been the gatekeepers of the community for many years. Although, in more recent years, that may be declining. This is because many young folks are not into organized religion. However, many people still seek out the pastors in their community or of their faith in times of need.

Faith leaders must become educated. They cannot make a person feel like it is a sin to suffer from depression or mental illness. There are many strategies pastors and others can use to help reduce the stigma of mental health disorders.

**Strategies for faith leaders and the community of faith to reduce stigma on mental health include:**

Resistance from seeking help may come from several places, from people who may be experiencing some behavioral issues. It is a belief held by many who will not ask for help because:

- Stigma associated with mental health. People are afraid to be labeled as strange. They also don't want to expose family members for fear of alienation.

- They are not comfortable acknowledging they have a problem. To say it may make it too real for the person.

- Feelings of hopelessness. 'There's no help available for me. I will never be normal,' which is what some may believe.

They may have some religious issues with mental health issues and what folks think about those who are suffering. There are those in the church who label people who are suffering from mental illness as "folks who are demons." Would you want people to think you are possessed by the devil? Conversations linking individuals with the devil is why many stay silent.

It's a cultural issue. African Americans have been taught not to tell people about their family business. "Keep our mess in the house."

As faith leaders, they have to be ready when people walk into the door needing and wanting help. Faith leaders have to become knowledgeable about resources and what to do to help those suffering.

There are several strategies that can be used to help the members and communities. Faith communities are charged to be supportive to those who are physically and mentally sick. What can they do as leaders?

1. Learn about mental illness.

- Take the Mental Health First Aid Training so you will understand what is happening and how to help. You can find out more information at this link: https://www.mentalhealthfirstaid.org/cs/

- Read books on the topic.

- Visit websites with valuable information.

- Invite presenters to speak to your church family.

2. Continue to discuss this topic with the household or the person and help them to understand the barriers.

- Make your faith community environment welcoming.

- Present a message on mental health issues.

- Have a workshop on your church site about mental illness.

3. Use stories of those who have come through similar situations, and help this person realize they are not alone.

- Introduce them to individuals who have recovered. There are many people willing to share their stories and are living a good life because they are taking their medications and understanding their illness.

- Find and review movies you can share on the topics that

show how to get help and allow people to see themselves in the characters.

4. Reassure people that they will and can get better.

- Connect them to places like NAMI (National Alliance on Mental Illness) and their Sharing Hope Group.

- Give them resources they can contact like: Behavioral Health Response. http://bhrstl.org/

5. Get the person involved. Ask if they are a person of faith and how faith can give them the strength to take steps toward healing.

Remember, mental health disorders are nothing to be ashamed of, and it is a medical problem - just like heart disease or diabetes.

An educated faith community can save the lives of so many desperate youths who are seeking comfort and consolation. Suicide shouldn't be a dirty word in church that is only mentioned with condemnation. Instead, we must embrace the concept that when one of us hurts, we all hurt.

## Chapter 9

## THE IMPACT OF SUICIDE & HOW WE CAN HELP

Unfortunately, young people who experience depression may have a desire to kill themselves. One study found that among black youth, 3.2% reported some suicidal thoughts in the past year; 1.4% reported attempting suicide (Joe et al., 2009). This may seem like a small number. However, suicide is the third leading cause of death among black youth (Lincoln et al., 2012).

Researchers have also found that suicide rates have doubled for black children, while declining for white children. They were surprised by their own results. This is the first recorded data in history for which black suicide rates surpass that of other race groups.

## The Suicide Rate For Black Children Is On The Rise

Suicide rate, per 1 million, for children aged 5-11 years in the U.S.

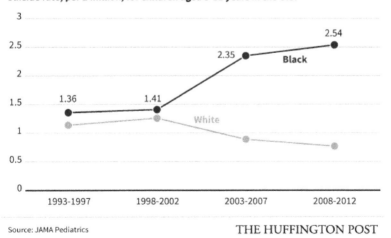

Source: JAMA Pediatrics                    THE HUFFINGTON POST

If you hear someone say they are going to kill themselves, believe them. Do not take their words lightly.

Be aware of the warning signs that can include but are not

limited to the following:

Talking about wanting to die or kill themselves

Looking for a way to kill themselves, (searching online or buying a gun

Talking about feeling hopeless or having no reason to live

Talking about feeling trapped or in unbearable pain

Talking about being a burden to others

Increasing the use of alcohol or drugs

Acting anxious or agitated; behaving recklessly

Sleeping too little or too much

Withdrawing or isolating themselves

Showing rage or talking about seeking revenge

Extreme mood swings

If you research this issue, you will find evidence that will demonstrate when you show concern, provide support to someone thinking of harming themselves, or even reduce their access to means of self-harm, these things will help to prevent one from dying by the hand of suicide. In addition, it is important to follow-up and check on your love ones to assure they are fine and if not, you can assist them further by calling the suicide hotline for more guidance. The number is 1-800-273-8255.

- There are many reasons a young person may want to die.

- They may feel as if they are a burden to others

- They are unhappy

- They are tired of being sad or living in their circumstance

- They feel hopeless

- They believe the problem is too big to fix

- They do not believe things will improve

The truth is, many youths who are feeling hopeless or who say they are going to kill themselves, do not want to die. They are tired of feeling depressed or losing hope and want to stop the sadness they feel.

If a youth feels like killing themselves, please encourage them to talk to someone right away. There are people who are trained that can help them. Encourage them to reach out to their teachers, pastors, counselors, and principals. It is important that youth do not allow their feelings to stay bottled up inside and keep the pain pent-up.

If they do, it could be like a bottle filled with pressure, ready to explode. Releasing the tension will ease the pressure inside. If you shake a bottle of soda before you open it, the contents inside will fizzle its way to the top, and when the cap is removed, everything in it will bubble quickly to the top, releasing the contents everywhere. It's like a volcano. That's how it is for many youths. When they are hurting inside, and they allow the pain to go unresolved, everyday life continues to pile more and more on them, and eventually, they will burst with emotion.

Talking about their feelings may be hard for some youth. They might have the following thoughts:

- I'm tired of feeling sad and I have thoughts about dying. What should I do?

- My life isn't worth living. I'm hurting inside. Can you help me feel better?

- There are times I feel like hurting myself and I need help. Would you help me?

- I need to talk to someone I can trust. I feel so hopeless. Will you help me?

- Letting a youth know that they expressed themselves to you and that you are concern and want to help may be a significant relief to them.

Remember, even though people talk about suicide, they may not want to die. They want to feel better but may feel as if suicide is their only option. We can help if we listen and allow them to speak. Once we do this, it's important to connect them to someone skilled in this field that can help.

There are many organizations and hotlines available to help. If a young person is suicidal, call the National Suicide Prevention Lifeline at **1-800-273-TALK (8255).** The National Suicide Prevention Lifeline is a national network of local crisis centers that provide free and confidential emotional support to people in suicidal crisis or emotional distress 24 hours a day, 7 days a week.

## What Happens When a Person Calls the Lifeline?

- First, you will hear a message telling you that you' have reached the National Suicide Prevention Lifeline.

- A skilled, trained crisis worker who works at the Lifeline Network crisis center closest to you will answer the phone.

- This person will listen to you, understand how your problem is affecting you, provide support, and share any resources that may be helpful.

If you cannot remember this number, just call 911. Immediately, you will be connected to someone who can help you.

Youth should not suffer in silence. Encourage them to talk to someone they trust, like a parent, teacher, or another responsible adult. There are people out there who want to help them feel better. They are just a phone call away. Let youth know these four, powerful words: **You are not alone.** Help is available. In the next chapter, you will learn how to help a young person in crisis.

# Chapter 10

## YOUTH IN CRISIS FROM YOUTH AND PARENTAL PERSPECTIVE

*What to do to help teens deal with depression:*

There are many organizations that work with teenagers. They should incorporate depression and other mental health issues into their curriculum or activities. Since too many kids are unwilling to discuss their personal situations, we must provide enough information to make them aware of why it is necessary to seek healthcare professionals when they are feeling at their lowest.

Education is the key to making positive changes in our lives. For too many years, we have believed in some stigmas that are simply not healthy for us. In many instances, some have accepted that having a mental illness means you are *crazy* or have *lost your m*arbles. There are many derogatory names associated with mental illness. Labels like: 'she rides the short, yellow, school bus', or the person is 'two French fries short of a Happy Meal' are often given. People can come up with all kinds of terminology to make a person feel bad about their situation.

It's important to discuss mental health and why there is no reason to be ashamed to take care of your health. We must teach our children that an illness is an illness, and to respect people who are suffering. No teen should reject help due to embarrassment.

Make teens aware of the negative perceptions persons may have about mental illness and ask them what we should do to alleviate this attitude. Get them involved. Talk to them. Let them be a part of the solution. When kids become knowledgeable about things, they tend to do better.

Ask teens to tell you why they think getting help when they

feel bad is not a good thing to do. Let them share why they believe needing help means they are *crazy*. Talk about how African Americans had so many negative things against them, historically, that some felt there was no need to add something else. In addition, in many African-American homes, it was appropriate to keep the family business in the home. Encourage the young person to flesh out this question and get them to discuss this issue. You will learn a lot about why the youth refuse to seek counseling when needed. You will also learn a lot about what they hear, so you can dispel the rumors and myths.

As parents, we can all do something to help our troubled youth.

- Discuss depression with your child; do not wait until they suffer a loss.

- Communicate by asking them about their thoughts and feelings.

- Watch a movie or TV show that addresses mental illnesses and ask questions. For instance, you can ask the young person what would you do in a situation like that? What do you think? You have to start a dialogue. Our young folks need to be included in conversations to understand better mental illnesses and how they can be addressed.

- Involve young people in skits about mental illness with resolutions included. Inform the audience of resources available in the local area.

- Print out resource lists and make sure the teen can see them. If needed, they will know exactly what to do.

- If you are working in the field of mental health, facilitate presentations in schools and have honest dialogue with the students.

- Post positive flyers about depression with phone numbers on them in places where students gather.

- Distribute hotline numbers to young people and encourage them to call if they or a friend is depressed.

- Educate churches, schools, and local hangouts about depression in youth and what resources are available for them.

In the next few chapters, you will learn how the author, Jermine Alberty, assisted his son during a period of suicidal ideation and attempts and how you can assist a young person in a non-crisis or crisis situation by using an action plan with four major elements. These four elements are 1) **H**earing, 2) **E**ngaging, 3) **L**earning and 4) **P**lanning.

Individuals often do not intervene in crisis situations because either they do not know what to say or what to do. They may often be afraid that if they intervene they might make the situation worse. I know that was the case when my son was dealing with depression, anxiety, and thoughts of suicide. I knew that he needed help but I had to figure out what would be the appropriate approach to assist him and meet him where he was.

# Chapter 11

## CAN YOU HEAR YOU NOW?

I grew up in an era where the philosophy...the saying... the thought process was "Children are to be seen and not heard." Even though, for some in our modern age, this may sound like a philosophy, a belief, or even a practice of antiquity, we try our best to do a better job of hearing our youth. I believe there is still some residue of that philosophy...that belief... that practice of seeing children but not hearing children.

This particular philosophy could be something that was practiced by the general population; in particular, from an African-American perspective. It was a bedrock of how African-Americans kept children in order, and sometimes, it was used in the disciplining process when a child would try to plead his case to avoid being disciplined.

Children would not be heard as to why they may have done what they did. It was immediately assumed that the child was guilty. Can you believe that in America, even still, an African-American child can be presumed guilty and not given a chance to prove that they are innocent?

Growing up, you can imagine the anxiety, the depression that a child might feel when their voice is never allowed to be heard by those who are in authority. The ideal first step in an intervention strategy to deal with youth who are dealing with depression or other mental illnesses is to hear them out. Some may challenge and say, "Well, is it not just about hearing children but also listening to children?" I would say yes. Listening is an important concept. However, if I cannot even hear the young person, it is difficult for me to even listen to the young person.

The first thing is for us to attune our ears to hear what young people are saying to us. Hear those signs. Hear those symptoms that young people are expressing to us. When I say symptoms, whether it is in the mental health field or even in the physical health field, symptoms are how a person feels. Often, we can see a sign or sometimes see a symptom but the only way we can accurately understand what the symptom may be conveying is to ask the person what they are feeling. In turn, when asking what they are feeling, hear what they are saying. That's why I believe that hearing is a very powerful first step in the intervention to help young people.

Let me tell you a story about my son who experienced depression and anxiety. Being trained and being a trainer in an early intervention program called Mental Health First Aid, one would assume that if I saw signs of mental health challenges, and if I knew symptoms of mental health challenges, that I would easily be able to pick up that my son was in distress. The reality was, as a parent, I had a gut feeling that there was something not quite right. and I would ask questions to try to get to what I thought was wrong but my son would only tell me what he thought I wanted to hear, because he feared my response if he told me something that he thought I may not want to hear. What I didn't know is the image below is what was bottled up on the inside of my son.

Jerimiah D. Alberty

For individuals who are working with young people, I think it's important that we understand that young people have a perception of a list of things that adults want to hear. They will speak from that list of things that they think we want to hear. In the process of speaking from that list, they put themselves in the background and their voices are never heard because they only speak what they think we want to hear.

It wasn't until after my son's numerous suicide attempts (the first attempt was in November 2015), after an inpatient hospital stay, after counseling, after medication, while sitting in a Sonic drive-thru, that I was inspired. Being a person of faith, I would attribute that inspiration to God. There I was, being inspired while sitting in a Sonic drive-thru, because my son had come to a point where he would not eat anything but a bacon toaster and cran-apple juice.

I pulled into Sonic's carport and I said to him, "I believe that a part of your anxiety - that a part of your depression - is rooted in the fact and the expectation that you believe I want you to live up to. The son who you think I want you to be is not the son that you currently are. The wrestle, between being who you think I want you to be and being who you currently are, is increasing your anxiety. Not only is it increasing your anxiety, but because you are not able to live up to the expectation that you think I want you to live up to, it causes you to be depressed.

That was the breakthrough moment. It was in that moment that he was able to speak, not what he thought I wanted to hear, but speak his truth. When he was able to speak his truth, I was finally able to hear him.

As long as he was telling me what he thought I wanted to hear, I could not hear him. It wasn't until he felt that he had my permission for his truth to be heard that he was able to freely convey his feelings. Once I heard him, it confirmed many of my suspicions and concerns, and I was finally able to meet him where he was.

49

## Chapter 12

# TO ENGAGE OR NOT TO ENGAGE

Once I was able to hear my son's truth, it was then that I was able to engage him and meet him where he was. There is a saying in the Hebrew scripture that is attributed to the prophet Amos, and it says, *How can two walk together except they be agreed?* Another translation says, *How can two walk together except they have an appointment?*

I like these two translations because one tells me that the only way two people can walk together is if they have an agreement to walk together. It is not only an agreement to walk together, but there is some intentionality of walking together.

When you visit large cities like: Chicago, New York, or even Los Angeles, people find themselves walking together. Not walking together on purpose, but walking together because the streets are so full that there is no choice but to walk side-by-side with one another.

Sometimes, it may appear that the circumstances in our lives forces us to walk together because we have been crowded together based upon numerous circumstances.

Families most often walk together because they are in the same household. In that same household, they find themselves eating together and attending activities together. They are together but often they are not in agreement. They are walking together because they *have* to be together.

In those large cities like: Chicago, New York, and Los Angeles, people are walking together because they have to walk together in order to get to a destination. They may not be in agreement that they are walking together but they are. Not only are they walking together, but they are walking closely together.

Sometimes, teens have to be with their parents. They walk

with their parents, not because they necessarily want to but because they have no choice. They were born in that family and they must walk in that family.

Notice the scripture, *How can two walk together except they be agreed?* Often, what will happen is when the circumstance allows and there is no longer a compulsion that two must walk together, a person will split off and go their own path. When there is no longer a compulsion to engage one another, there is no longer a compulsion to walk together. Then, there's the other translation. The term *agreed* is used as an appointment, thus changing the translation to, *How can two walk together except they have an appointment?* The appointment means intentionality. The appointment means that two people have come together and agreed with intention to meet at a certain time.

That's why engagement is such an important strategy in helping a young person. As adults, we have to intentionally create appointed times where we talk with our young people and hear what they say. We have to find intentional times, appointed times to walk together, to be in fellowship together with them in order to hear what they are saying.

With my son and his depression, we had to create an intentional system where we engaged each other at appointed times to check=in and check on his well-being. Still being a high school student and dealing with the pressures of school, the pressures of social media, the pressures of his own illness, it created opportunities for anxiety and depression. Substance abuse, and self-injury were triggered. Now that we have crossed the hurdle - that he will not speak only what I want to hear but he will speak his truth so that he can be heard - the engagement between us is much easier.

We have no longer put in front of us the barrier of speaking half-truths or the barrier of speaking untruths. We have removed those barriers and we have said both ways, "I want to hear your truth. That truth will not always make us feel good but I want to hear your truth. And I will be honest with you when you speak your truth to me."

The system of engagement that we developed is a check-in system and we use technology. That technology is texting. It is used when he feels an episode of depression or an episode of anxiety is beginning.

We discussed risk factors and protector factors in the other chapters. You've learned about episodes already in previous chapters. You've learned that mental illness is not always a constant, static state in a person's life. You've learned that a person may experience episodes and those episodes can occur once or they can be recurrent.

Now that I could hear my son, it was important that we talked about how to engage each other when an episode was about to occur or when an episode *was* occurring. That system, using text messaging, was a way that we could do that.

The system was based on one to ten. If he was a nine, eight, or seven, those were good numbers. Those numbers meant, *I'm doing pretty good today*. The moment we got to six, five, or four, we knew by the system we set up, there was potential that he may need an intervention. He may need for me to come and sit with him. He may need to leave school and step away from that environment, so that it didn't escalate into something worse. We had the system, and we engaged each other through the system.

The system was not only for when there was an episode of depression or anxiety that may have been beginning; it was also a regular check-in system. I would text, "Hey, how are you doing today? What's your number?" Isn't it interesting that in this world of fitness and in this world that we give credence to numbers, that a wellness number can be so important?

Can you imagine, as adults, we created a system with young

people and we said, "For you who have been bullied, you who are under pressure to do different things that you just don't want to do. Hey! What's your number?" If they said, "I'm a nine today" or "I'm a four today" we would know what that number meant in order to intervene. That number meant to continue to provide support, or that number meant they are okay.

When we truly get through the barrier of being able to hear our youth's truth - whatever that may be - it will help us to be able to engage with them properly.

I think this is a good place to tell a story. When we talk about engaging youth properly, my son for example, as a way to deal with his issues, or to self-medicate, or even as a way to cope with his issues, my son would use drugs. In particular, marijuana. His therapist knew about this but because of confidentiality, she could not reveal this to me. It was in a conversation that my son and I had that I learned he was using marijuana. He was using it because he liked the way it made him feel.

I mentioned the therapist and how she knew my son was using drugs but could not reveal it to me. When I sat down with her for our one-on-one sessions to discuss my son's progress, I revealed to her that he told me. She was ecstatic because I knew, and because I now know the truth, we could partner together to address it.

She said something to me that startled me. She said, "You know, your son thinks that you are okay with him smoking marijuana." I was taken aback. What impression did I give him to think that I was okay with doing drugs? In my effort to meet him where he was; in my effort to speak truth to him, I never told him outright, "Don't do this!" I didn't think I had to. I had to understand that he didn't understand me clearly. I had to learn how he interpreted my cues. I had to learn how he interpreted what I was saying to help him in this intervention.

That's why it is so important that we learn from the young

person what we can do to help them, but also what we can do to ensure clarity of what we are saying and how we can be of assistance.

# Chapter 13

## LEARN FROM ME

The next part of the intervention is learning. We talked about how hearing individuals is important. Once we can truly hear a young person then we can engage the young person. We also talked about how learning about my son's truth helped me to better engage him. Some may ask, "Why isn't the next step listening?" And I would answer, "The only way you can learn from a person is to listen."

Think about the process. We hear the person, which enables us to engage the person and then learn from that person. The way we learn from that person is that we listen. Learning and listening goes hand in hand. It may be that through listening we learn, or that by learning we actually are able to listen.

When you think about different quotes you've heard over time about learning, one of the quotes you might hear about learning is from William Glasser......

*"Ten percent of what we read is how we learn. Twenty percent of what we hear is how we learn. Thirty percent of what we see is how we learn. Fifty percent of what we see and hear is how we learn. Seventy percent of what is discussed with others is how we learn. Eighty percent of what is experienced personally is how we learn. Ninety-five percent of what we teach to someone else is how we learn. It appears that the majority of this learning is rooted in what is experienced personally and in what we teach to someone else."*

What is important is that we listen to that personal experience from the young person in order to learn how to help them.

I am reminded of my son sharing with me about self-injury. Again, once we came into this truthful relationship and I was able to learn how to engage him, my concern was in regards to his self-injury.

Self-injurious behavior can result in one being in serious psychological distress. My goal was to stop his self-injury. What I failed to focus on was why he was self-injuring. I was trying to figure out how I could help him, but me trying to figure out how to help him was wrong. The reason I say it was wrong is because oftentimes, that's where the mistake lies. Instead of *asking* the person, we try to figure out on our own what we can do to help the person when we need to learn from them.

In my attempt to figure out how to help my son, my goal became to hide every sharp object in the house—and that is what I did. Then, I learned that even if I took away every sharp object in the house, he could still self-injure with a paperclip. Imagine how easily accessible a paper clip is at school. Imagine how easy it is to hide a paperclip.

Through my son I was able to learn how to assist him. It really wasn't about me stopping the self-injury, which was a result of his depression and his anxiety. It was about getting to the heart of why he self-injured.

Sometimes, I think that when we think about the importance of learning, we fail to realize what John Powell stated, *"The only real mistake is the one from which we learn nothing."*

As a parent, if I continue to force my opinion...if I continued to force how I wanted to engage and didn't learn from what I was being told, that is the mistake.

I think what is important in the process of engaging young people, is that we must understand that respect is key in this learning component. Sometimes as adults, we believe because we are adults that respect is something that should automatically be given to us. But, you've heard it before, *"Respect is earned."* As adults, it may be hard for many of us to understand that.

When we learn how to respect young people, that is when they can be honest with us. When we respect them and honesty is built, that's when we can gain an appreciation for honesty. Honesty breeds trust. The trust that is bred is a result of what was gained in the relationship. In that, we are able to create a relationship where there is a rapport that is built. A trust that is built will result in a sense of loyalty to that relationship.

This learning component is so very important because when we talk about how we are engaging young people, it's one of those things where we realize that in this process of engagement – in this process of learning how to engage – we all make mistakes. The important thing to understand is that we should learn from those mistakes.

Another important thing to understand in the learning process is that the most powerful thing we can give young people is *options*. I know that for many people the idea of giving young people options can be scary. The idea is that we are to give them directives, and as young people, they are to take those directives.

When dealing with depression and other illnesses, it can be difficult to take a directive and follow through with that directive. That is why it is so important that we understand - in this process - that by giving youth options it will empower them to be able to help us work with them in creating a plan. In order for the plan to be successful, it has to have their buy-in.

That's why I believe the quote from Benjamin Franklin is important: *"Tell me and I'll forget. Teach me and I'll remember. Involve me and I'll learn."*

# Chapter 14

## PUTTING IT IN ACTION - CREATING THE PLAN

Once you have heard the young person, engaged them, and learned from them, then and only then can you begin to create a plan. This plan must have the buy-in from the young person. The youth must feel that the plan is designed to empower them and not disempower them.

What is the difference between empowering and disempowering? To empower someone is when you give them the authority or power to do something. To disempower them is when you tell them what they *should* be doing. Therefore, it is important when you create the plan that it includes what the youth *could* do and not what the youth *should* do.

What is the difference between *could* and *should*? When you let a youth know what they could do, you are providing them information that leads to options or choices. When you tell a youth what they should be doing, you are offering your advice, which typically begins with the words "If I were you I would...," or "I think you should...."

When youth are dealing with depression, mustering the energy to act requires an inner strength. It is important that when you plan with the youth that you do not allow the myth that for many years have kept people from seeking help. That myth is that *depression is due to a personal weakness or lack of willpower*. Many people think that a depressed person can simply "snap out of it" by using willpower; however, this is NOT true!

Help the youth create a plan that includes goals that they can accomplish and not become frustrated when they do not come to pass. It is important that youth create SMART goals that give them clarity and a deadline for achieving them.

The basic definition of SMART goals includes these elements:

They are **specific**. The goal should be clearly defined. It should also be **measurable.** The youth needs to be able to quantify the goal so they know they can achieve it. The goal should be **attainable.** It is good for them to set goals that will stretch and challenge them, but they need to make sure that they do not create a goal that will lead to frustration and failure. The goal should also be **relevant**. The youth's goals should fit within their ultimate plans in life. Lastly, the goal should be **time-bound.** The youth needs to set a date by which their goal will be achieved.

Once the youth has completed their plan and their goals, your role is to simply be an encourager and help lead the young person. John Maxwell said it best: "If you are a leader, you should never forget that everyone needs encouragement. And everyone who receives it - young or old, successful or less-than-successful, unknown or famous - is changed by it."

We hope this book has encouraged you that you can make a difference in the life of young person. Remember, one of the most powerful protective factors in the life of a youth is a caring adult! If you are concerned don't hesitate to reach out and help. We charge you to spread the good news that "Recovery is Possible".

If you are a young person who has read this book, we want to encourage you to ask for help. Remember there are adults who care about your well-being and desire that you prosper and be in good health.

# CASE STUDY 1

Jim decided he was unhappy with his school and was tired of people laughing at his clothes. He was from a family of little means, and his mother could not afford to buy him things that other kids had. Every day, when he arrived to school, the kids would gather, point at his cheap shoes and clothes, and laugh and tease him. It was torture. He could no longer concentrate, and his straight A grades plummeted to D's and F's.

He walked around with his head hung to the ground. He couldn't find the energy to smile. He shied away from students and adults. Life was too hard.

He grew tired of being the butt of jokes and hearing people laughing and discussing him. He was only 14 years old, but he felt old and tired. He did not want to live because he felt his mom was doing all she could to take care of her children on her small salary, and he did not want to be a burden on her any longer. He decided tonight was the night he would end it all.

How would you **H.E.L.P.** Jim?

**Case Study 1**

# H.E.L.P. INTERVENTION

What do you hear Jim saying?

_____
_____
_____

How might you engage Jim?

_____
_____
_____

What did you learn about Jim?

_____
_____
_____

What would be your plan to assist Jim?

_____
_____
_____

# CASE STUDY 2

Terrance had life in the palm of his hands. He wore the best clothes and shoes that money could buy. His dad was a drug dealer who gave his son any and everything he wanted. Terrance walked around happy and felt on top of the world. He never dreamed his world would come tumbling down.

One day, when he arrived home from school, he saw police cars everywhere. As he neared his home, the 13-year-old boy was hurt by what he saw. His father was laying on the ground with his hands cuffed behind his back. The closer he tried to get to his dad, the police officers made him get back.

The officers were bringing furniture and other appliances like televisions and computers from his house. Yellow, caution tape surrounded their home. He saw his grandmother, who grabbed his arm and pulled him to her old, tattered-looking car.

His father was arrested and eventually sentenced to 10 years in prison. Terrance was devastated. He had nowhere to go but to his granny's house.

Once he moved in with his beautiful clothes and shoes, his uncle, who was a drug addict, began stealing his clothing and expensive tennis shoes. Before long, he had nothing. He cried on his granny's shoulder, but she was old and could not do anything to help.

Days passed. He and his granny could barely find enough to eat because his uncle was stealing the food and selling it. Terrance wanted to give up. He thought death would ease his pain. He missed his dad, and he loved his granny, but he knew she would do better if she could. He stayed in his room and cried. After all, teenagers like him who had everything when others had nothing should feel embarrassed now that he had joined the same kids he once spent time teasing.

How would you **H.E.L.P.** Terrance?

**Case Study 2**

# H.E.L.P. INTERVENTION

What do you *hear* Terrance saying?

_____

_____

_____

How might you *engage* Terrance?

_____

_____

_____

What did you *learn* about Terrance?

_____

_____

_____

What would be your *plan* to assist Terrance?

_____

_____

_____

# CASE STUDY 3

Amber cried every day. She prayed and asked God to save her but God was taking too long. She didn't know how much longer she could keep away from those dirty men her drug-addicted mom brought to the house.

Amber was a beautiful, young girl. Her body had developed in the right places, causing her to look older than she was. She didn't focus on her beauty; she focused on what was inside of her. What lived inside of her was an intelligent and smart young woman who aspired to become an educated and trained doctor. Amber would help her mother become clean and live the best life ever.

First, Amber had to keep the dirty men from raping her. Every night, she would go to sleep with three pairs of blue jeans on and three pairs of underwear. Then, she would zip herself tightly into her sleeping bag. She also kept a knife inside the bag with her.

She was so tired of fighting the men away and screaming. There were days she would arrive at school sleepy, after keeping her eyes open to protect her virginity. She couldn't take it anymore. Her tears fell continuously, and she needed help. She knew the moment she told what was happening, the system would move her into one of those foster homes where several of her friends had already been raped by the men in the house they were assigned. If she couldn't be a doctor, she would rather be dead.

How would you **H.E.L.P.** Amber?

**Case Study 3**

# H.E.L.P. INTERVENTION

What do you *hear* Amber saying?

_____

_____

_____

How might you *engage* Amber?

_____

_____

_____

What did you *learn* about Amber?

_____

_____

_____

What would be your *plan* to assist Amber?

_____

_____

_____

# CASE STUDY 4

Cynthia couldn't go to school without being bullied, daily. The kids teased her about her skin color. She was a beautiful, dark skin girl. Others saw her as dirty, ugly, and too dark. Her mother told her she was gorgeous and not to listen to the kids. Daily, they called her names like darky, black and ugly, midnight, and other names that made her feel bad.

Cynthia tried to listen to her mom and believe the words she said to make her feel better. Nothing seemed to help. She was tired of the teasing, tired of hiding from others until she decided enough was enough.

Cynthia loved her parents and tried hard to accept the things she could not change and be happy. That was hard to do when others received joy from making her feel bad.

One day, Cynthia cleared out her locker, wrote a note to her family, and entered the home she had lived in for 13 years. She put the letter on the table, by her mother's phone, to make sure she saw it. She went to her room and tried to kill herself by taking a bottle of pills.

What signs did Cynthia give to let her mother know she needed help?

How would you **H.E.L.P.** Cynthia?

**Case Study 4**

# H.E.L.P. INTERVENTION

What do you *hear* Cynthia saying?

_____

_____

_____

How might you *engage* Cynthia?

_____

_____

_____

What did you *learn* about Cynthia?

_____

_____

_____

What would be your *plan* to assist Cynthia?

_____

_____

_____

# CASE STUDY 5

"Jerry, you are a dummy. You make me sick, with your slow self. You can't read, just like your mama." It was hard to make it through one day without being called names. Jerry was not dumb. He had a difficult time reading because he did not have anyone to help him with his homework. He was trying hard, but the words were difficult.

Jerry would come home and tell his mother what the kids said and did to him. She told him he had to learn how to fight back. His mother said, "When you knock one child out, the others will leave you alone." Jerry didn't want to hurt others. He knew how it felt to have pain piercing your heart daily. He wasn't the type of child who wanted to fight.

He was a 12-year-old boy whose mother was a former drug user. He didn't know his father, and whenever he asked his mother about his dad, she said she was his daddy and that he shouldn't miss what he never had. He missed not having a dad. He believed if he had a dad, the kids would not tease him. He became tired and decided to take things into his own hands. The tears were drying up, his head hurt all the time, and he couldn't sleep. One morning, after spending a restless night crying, he dressed, went into the kitchen, picked out the sharpest knife he could find, put it into his book bag, and went to school. After that day, no other kid would have the courage to bully him again.

What should his mother have done to help Jerry?

**Case Study 5**

# H.E.L.P. INTERVENTION

What do you *hear* Jerry saying?

_____

_____

_____

How might you *engage* Jerry?

_____

_____

_____

What did you *learn* about Jerry?

_____

_____

_____

What would be your *plan* to assist Jerry?

_____

_____

_____

In writing this book, our goal was to enlighten and educate

people about trauma, mental health and to help to reduce the stigma of mental health. We know through our experiences, education, and research that recovery is possible. We believe that with the appropriate help, a person who is suffering can have a better life. We dedicate this book to you the reader, those who are suffering and to all the organizations that provide resources to help.

# RESOURCES TO HELP!

## Depression Related Organizations/Sites

<u>National Suicide Prevention Lifeline</u> – Only federally-funded national hotline. Provides a 24-hour, toll-free, confidential crisis hotline for anyone (you or a loved one) who may be suicidal or in psychological crisis. Calls are routed to the nearest available crisis center in your area. Get immediate suicide crisis support, mental health information, and referrals to services in your area.

Suicide/Crisis Hotline: (800) 273-TALK (8255)

Hotline for Spanish Speakers: (888) 628-9454

TTY Hotline: (800) 799-4TTY (4889)

<u>National Hope Line Network</u> – Provides a national, 24-hour, toll-free suicide prevention hotline. Your call will be connected to the nearest certified crisis center. You can also search for a crisis center nearest you in their online directory.

<u>Suicide Hotline: (800)-SUICIDE (784-2433)</u>

Kristin Brooks Hope Center
615 7th Street NE
Washington, DC 20002
Phone: 202.536.3200
Email (General Comments):
info@hopeline.com

<u>National Institute of Mental Health (NIMH)</u> – Federal agency that provides mental health information, supports, and conducts research on mental and behavioral disorders.

National Institute of Mental Health (NIMH)
Public Information and Communications Branch

6001 Executive Boulevard, Room 8184, MSC 9663
Bethesda, MD 20892-9663
Main Local: (301) 443-4513
Main Toll-Free: (866) 615-6464
TTY Local: (301) 443-8431
TTY Toll-Free: (866) 415-8051
Fax: (301) 443-4279
Email: nimhinfo@nih.gov

National Alliance on Mental Illness (NAMI) – Largest national grassroots organization dedicated to improving the lives of people with mental illness and their families. Provides support, education, advocacy, and research for people living with mental illness. Local chapters in every state.

2107 Wilson Blvd., Suite 300
Arlington, VA 22201-3042
Phone: (703) 524-7600
TDD: (703)-516-7227
Fax: (703) 524-9094
Help Line: 800-950-NAMI (6264)
Email: info@nami.org

Mental Health American (formerly known as National Mental Health Association) – One of the nation's leading non-profit organizations committed to helping all people have better mental health. Provides advocacy and information on mental health disorders, treatment, tests and screenings and where to get help.

Mental Health America

2000 N. Beauregard Street, 6th Floor
Alexandria, Virginia 22311
Main: (703) 684-7722
Main Toll-Free: (800) 969-6MHA (6642)

TTY: (800) 433-5959
Fax: (703) 684-5968
Crisis Line: (800) 273-TALK (8255)
Email: Form on site

Depression and Bipolar Support Alliance (DBSA) – Nation's leading non-profit organization supporting individuals with depression and bipolar disorder. DBSA has an 800 information and referral line, over 1,000 support groups nationwide, educational materials and programs. DBSA also supports research and promotes advocacy for people living with mood disorders.

Depression and Bipolar Support Alliance

730 N. Franklin Street, Suite 501
Chicago, Illinois 60610-7224
Toll-free: (800) 826-3632
Fax: (312) 642-7243

Email: info@dbsalliance.org

American Foundation for Suicide Prevention – National organization focused on the prevention of suicide. Provides education and research grants, programs for individuals surviving loss from suicide and advocacy for legislation to further research and suicide prevention. Has local chapters across the country.

American Foundation for Suicide Prevention

120 Wall Street, 22nd Floor
New York, NY 10005
Toll-free: (888) 333-AFSP
Phone: (212) 363-3500
Fax: (212) 363-6237
Email: inquiry@afsp.org

American Association of Suicidology (AAS) – Founded in 1968, a not-for-profit organization dedicated to the understanding and prevention of suicide. AAS promotes research, provides publications, public education, and awareness, training to professionals and support groups for survivors. AAS is a national clearinghouse for information on suicide.

American Association of Suicidology

5221 Wisconsin Avenue, NW
Washington, DC 20015
Phone: (202) 237-2280
Fax: (202) 237-2282
Email: info@suicidology.org

Read a chapter of A Hole in My Heart by Rose Jackson-Beavers and her nephew, Edward Booker. The individual in this story sought counseling and is living in recovery.

# A HOLE IN MY HEART

### Chapter 1

"Somebody, please help me! Please, help me!" pleaded Adrienne. "Help me! Please, save my baby! Please!" she sobbed.

Adrienne raced down the quiet street with her baby in her arms. She quickly flung young Darrius, her small, bundle of joy, over her shoulder, no longer able to stand to look into his wide, clear eyes while he struggled to breathe.

Darrius was only 17 months old, and he had joyfully crawled around on the floor for more than 30 minutes under the watchful eyes of his loving mother. Giggling, he pulled his small body up on the glass and cherry wood coffee table and reached for a piece of hard candy.

Adrienne never saw the candy, as the ringing telephone had suddenly distracted her. While she talked to the sales clerk on the phone, she noticed that her inquisitive child had become very quiet - almost eerily quiet. Too silent! Scary!

She hung the phone up quickly and called out Darrius' name. There was no sound. No laughter. Only the echoes of her now, too timid voice calling for the child who made her whole. He was the little boy who had given her a reason to live, a reason to breathe.

She ran quickly through the kitchen to the living room and saw his body. He was lying on his back with a hazed look in his eyes. Small breaths were seeping through his mouth. He was begging her with his body to help him breathe.

She grabbed him and flung open the door to find help. Seeing none, she took off running as fast as Marion Jones did in the 100-metre dash. She had to find help. Fast!

As tears streamed down her caramel-colored skin, she pleaded for someone to save her child. With her baby laid gently over her shoulder, she started to stumble. Trying desperately to secure her hold on her son, she grabbed him tightly across his stomach.

This was the act that saved her child's life. It was when she grabbed him around his mid-section to soften the fall that she saw a small piece of candy pop out of his mouth and he started to breathe. She was so thankful! She kissed her baby on the cheek and silently thanked God for saving her only child. As she looked at his tiny feet and hands, giving him a once-over to assure herself that he was okay, she let the tears roll down her face and drip on the prettiest and sweetest baby she had ever seen.

Adrienne Genise was the middle child and second daughter of Elizabeth and Jasper McMillan's clan of five. She was the most sensitive of the group. Always trying to find love in the wrong places, she often found herself in situations that were not conducive to maintaining her self-esteem. Even though her parents tried to show her how much she was loved, she always seemed to seek more than they could give.

When Adrienne became pregnant, her parents were not angry. Previously, she had tried to commit suicide and was diagnosed with depression. Thinking that her pregnancy would help her, they celebrated the news with her. During the pregnancy, her life changed.

No longer depressed, she prepared for the birth of her child while she shopped for everything that the newborn would need.

Everyone who knew Adrienne felt that she was a great mother. She never left her child, but always stayed by his side. She kept him clean and fed. She doted on her baby, constantly kissing and hugging him. After the birth of her second child, two years later, her life could not have been happier. Her relationship with her children was strong and based on pure love.

Little Darrius and his sister, Jacqui, were happy children. Darrius' life was almost perfect, until he was six years old. Then, in the blink of an eye, his mother changed from always being by his side to missing in action.

## Chapter 2

"Nathan, what are you gonna do today? Let's go swimming in Old Man Kemon's pool," said Darrius.

"You know that crabby dude ain't gone let us swim. And besides, I have to get back home to help my mom with yard work."

"Well, I'll catch you later." Darrius walked away and suddenly turned around and called out to his friend. "Nathan, man," he said. "You sure are lucky that you have parents who care."

"Man, don't go and get sentimental on me. You have people who have your back - like your granny."

"Yea, dude. But I'd rather have my mom living with us, and I would like to at least know my father."

"Ask your mom to tell you who he is. Then, you can come by the house, and we can search the Net to see if we can find him," Nathan said, encouragingly.

"I'll try, but you know my moms! When she's using that stuff, she be tripping; and when she need that stuff and can't get it, she is worse. So, I basically try to give her a little let lone. But if she comes by Granny's house today, I will ask. I'll see you later. Bring your basketball and let's hoop."

"Later, man."

Darrius Jay McMillan was a medium-sized, straight A student with a walnut complexion. He was well-mannered; but as quickly as a tiger sneaks up on its prey, he could change into a child with delinquent behavior. He was angry at the world but didn't understand how to handle it. Rather than taking it out on the person who made him angry, he allowed it to fester and rumble until it became like a volcano about to erupt. His heart ached so badly that only something very strong could soothe his bruised and damaged soul. It was as if he had gas in his chest that needed full-strength Pepto-Bismol.

Darrius was active in church and participated in a group called the Spirited Kids. He was a member of their exclusive marching team, which had won trophies and accolades across the country. He was a premium stepper who often carried the flag or played the drums while performing.

Whatever he set his mind to do, he did it. He made sure that it was top-of-the-line quality. He was only 13 years old and in the eighth grade, but he had already won as many trophies as his granny had forks and spoons in her kitchen drawer. Yet, he was so sad.

Often, Darrius found himself not wanting to do anything except talk to his aunt, Javia. She was the one person who understood him. Although she was 40 years old, she was as smart as Bill Gates and as generous as Oprah Winfrey, and just as precious.

He often wondered: *Why couldn't God have given her to me as my mother*? He wanted a connection with his mom, but he knew that it would take as many prayers as fish in all the ocean to secure the response he so desperately wanted from God.

His aunt was special. She was older than his mom, Adrienne, who was just turning 29. Javia was special because she had always wanted children but didn't have any of her own, so she lavished a lot of love on the children she knew in church, at work and in her family. She was considerate because she knew that Darrius needed his mom. She gave him more attention than a battalion of military soldiers gave when saluting their superiors.

Javia was also born on the same day as Darrius - July 5th, but 28 years earlier. His mom did not have anything in common with her sister, except that they had the same mom and dad. Adrienne was argumentative and irresponsible, and she often cursed. She used drugs and alcohol, as if she needed them to sustain her life and to make Darrius and his 10-year-old sister, Jacqui, miserable.

"Little punk! Come here right now," screamed Adrienne.

"What did I do now?" asked Darrius.

"Didn't I tell you to wash Granny's dishes? Boy, don't let me knock the stank out of your butt!"

"Why do you have to put me down? I didn't do anything."

Adrienne reached out and hit Darrius in the back with her fist. "Don't talk back to me. Get your nappy, tight head out of my face."

Darrius walked toward the kitchen with tears streaming down his face. Sometimes, Darrius hated her and wished that she was not his mother. He wished he knew who his daddy was. He'd asked her so many times, but she ignored him or lied and told him that he and Jacqui had the same dad.

He knew she was lying because Matt, Jacqui's dad, never even acknowledged him when he came over to pick her up for the weekend. Plus, his mother had named him after another man, before she admitted to everyone that she didn't know who his dad was, because she was high at the time that he was conceived. This just made him even angrier. How in the world could she have a child when she acted like one herself?

Now, he lived with his grandma, Elizabeth. Unfortunately, his mother sometimes showed up to try to run his life, as if the courts had never terminated her parental rights over him and Jacqui. Fortunately, he only had to deal with her on those days, and then she would disappear until the next time she wanted to show her motherly concern for her children...the ones she refused to release to another woman, no matter what the court said.

## Rose Jackson-Beavers Bio 2017

*Rose Jackson-Beavers, Chief Executive Officer of Prioritybooks Publications grew up in East St. Louis, Illinois and received her Bachelor and Master degrees from Illinois State and Southern Illinois Universities. Rose is an inspirational speaker who is frequently asked to talk to youths and young adults about life issues. She has worked with many teens throughout her community and has received numerous awards and recognition for her work in youth empowerment and publishing.*

*She has worked as a freelance writer for A-Magazine, a St. Louis Publication, and The Spanish Lake Word Newspaper and as an Opinion Shaper for the North County Journal Newspaper. Married for thirty-three years to Cedric, they have one daughter, Adeesha. Rose is the author of ten books. Her 2012 book, A Sinner's Cry was a finalist in the Religious Fiction category of, The Next Generation Indie Book Awards 2012. Rose is an Amazon bestselling author. She has published over thirty authors and more than 100 books with many of the books becoming best sellers and receiving award-winning recognition. Visit her website at http://www.prioritybooks.com/ or from http://www.amazon.com/ or http://www.barnesandnoble.com/. She can be reached at rosbeav03@yahoo.com, or at 314-306-2972. You can also visit her on her Facebook page at https://www.facebook.com/rose.jacksonbeavers.*

### BOOKS FOR YOUNG PEOPLE

Caught in the Net of Deception

A Hole in My Heart (pt. 1)

A Holiday Wish (pt. 2)

### <u>Social Media Contacts:</u>

http://instagram.com/rosejacksonbeavers

https://www.facebook.com/rose.jacksonbeavers

https://www.facebook.com/prioritybookspublications

www.rosejacksonbeavers.com

www.prioritybooks.com

www.prioritybooks.blogspot.com

## Rev. Jermine D. Alberty, BSB/M, M. Div. Bio 2018

Jermine D. Alberty, M. Div. has dedicated his life to the service of others. He truly believes that to be the "salt of the earth" that we must serve, affirm, and love each other. He believes that through these actions, a transformation will take place in the hearts of individuals and communities.

Alberty, completed a bachelor's degree in business with an emphasis in management from the University of Phoenix. In 2012, he received his Master of Divinity degree at Central Baptist Theological Seminary.

For the past 25 years, he has served in both faith-based and secular capacities, including non-profits, faith communities, government, mental health, and academia. He has served in the roles as a community organizer, planning assessment team training director for a community mental health center, a principal investigator with the University of Missouri St. Louis. As a National Trainer of Mental Health First Aid he has trained hundreds of instructors and thousands of first aiders.

Alberty currently serves as the Executive for Pathways to Promise an interfaith cooperative of many faith groups, which reaching out to those with mental illnesses and their families. He possesses a deep passion for mental health ministry through personal experience with love ones he has cared for through their journey of recovery.

Jermine is the husband of Dyyone Alberty and they have been married for 22 years. He is also the father of three young adults Dominique, Jer'Mia and Jerimiah.

# References

1  Kessler, R. C.; Berglund, P.; Demler, O.; Jin, R.; Walters, E. E. 2005. Life-time Prevalence and Age-of-onset Distribution of DSM-IV Disorders in the National Co-morbidity Survey Replication. Archives of General Psychiatry 62: 593-602

2  https://www.nami.org/Learn-More/Mental-Health-Conditions

3  http://www.fultoncountyga.gov/bhdd-symptoms-a-warning-signs

4  http://www.mentalhealthamerica.net/recognizing-warning-signs

5  http://www.mentalhealthamerica.net/recognizing-warning-signs

6  http://www.mentalhealthamerica.net/recognizing-warning-signs

7  National Institute of Mental Health

8  Center for Mental Health Services, U.S. Department of Health and Human Services. (1996)

9  National Institute of Mental Health, "Depression research at the National Institute of Mental Health," updated April 13, 1999.

10  American Academy of Child and Adolescent Psychiatry: "The Depressed Child." Facts for Families Fact Sheet Series, Accessed Sept. 1999.

11  Joe, S., Baser, R. S., Neighbors, H. W., Caldwell, C. H., & Jackson, J. S. (2009). 12-month and lifetime prevalence of suicide attempts among black adolescents in the National Survey of American Life. Journal of the American Academy of Child & Adolescent Psychiatry, 48(3), 271-282.

12   Lincoln, K. D., Taylor, R. J., Chatters, L. M., & Joe, S. (2012). Suicide, negative interaction and emotional support among black Americans. Social psychiatry and psychiatric epidemiology, 47(12), 1947-1958.

13   http://www.depression-help-resource.com/types-of-depression.htm

14   http://www.depression-help-resource.com/types-of-depression.htm

15   http://www.depression-help-resource.com/types-of-depression.htm

16   http://www.depression-help-resource.com/types-of-depression.htm

17   http://www.depression-help-resource.com/types-of-depression.htm

18   http://www.depression-help-resource.com/types-of-depression.htm

19   http://www.depression-help-resource.com/types-of-depression.htm

20   O'Connell, M. E., Boat, T., & Warner, K. E.. (2009). Preventing mental, emotional, and behavioral disorders among young people: Progress and possibilities.

21   http://www.apa.org/topics/trauma/

22   O'Connell, M. E., Boat, T., & Warner, K. E.. (2009). Preventing mental, emotional, and behavioral disorders among young people: Progress and possibilities.

CPSIA information can be obtained
at www.ICGtesting.com
Printed in the USA
LVHW011340261118
598272LV00002B/126/P

9 780979 282317